Finding the Fit

Helping Clients Clarify MBTI® Type

Sally Carr

About the Author

Sally Carr has worked for OPP for nine years. She uses the MBTI in team-building, individual development and leadership training. She is a member of the Training Faculty of the Association for Psychological Type and has taught on the MBTI Qualifying Workshop since 1990. Sally's preferences are for ESTP.

Acknowledgments

This booklet draws together ideas and tips borrowed from many colleagues and clients. I would particularly like to thank Susan Brock for the encouragement she gave me to persist with the project; Jean Kummerow, Naomi Quenk and Betsy Kendall for their useful suggestions; Ann O'Sullivan for the quote on page 6.

Finally, Catherine Fitzgerald for helping me "find the fit" for myself, thereby bringing the MBTI alive for me.

Contents

Introduction 3
Basic Assumptions 4
Steps in Giving Feedback 5
Cautions 6
Questions to Ask, Strategies to Follow 8
The Strategies in Action 9
Case Examples 18
Conclusion 23
References 24

Copyright © 1997 by OPP Ltd. All rights reserved. Published by OPP Ltd, Elsfield Hall, 15-17 Elsfield Way, Oxford, OX2 8EP, England. First published 1997. No portion of this publication may be reproduced, stored in a retrieval system, or transmitted in any form or by any means, electronic, mechanical, photocopying, recording or otherwise, without prior written permission of the publisher. No part of this booklet is reproducible under any photocopying licence scheme. This booklet is excluded from the Copyright Licensing Agency Rapid Clearance Service (CLARCS).

®MBTI, Myers-Briggs Type Indicator and the MBTI logo are trade marks or registered trade marks of the Myers-Briggs Type Indicator Trust in the United States and other countries. OPP Ltd is the exclusive licensee of the trade marks in the UK.
®Introduction to Type is a registered trade mark of the Myers-Briggs Type Indicator Trust. OPP Ltd is the exclusive distributor of the MBTI in the UK and Ireland.

Cartoons by Val Saunders.

OPP Ltd
Elsfield Hall
15-17 Elsfield Way
Oxford
OX2 8EP
Tel: 01865 404500
Fax: 01865 557483

ISBN 1 85639 096 9

®OPP and the OPP logo are registered trade marks of OPP Ltd.

Introduction

This booklet has been inspired by the experiences of newly qualified users of the MBTI®. Over and over again, when I ask where they would like more help, they respond:

> "How can I help people who are unsure of their type preferences?"

I'm always pleased to hear the question, because it shows that the person has understood the importance of allowing clients to decide for themselves where they fit into the type framework. They recognise that reported type is only a hypothesis, and that the individual is the best judge of their type. But when people say things like...

> "Well I do both, I can see myself in both – I can't decide which is more like me."

> "When you described the preferences I thought I was a Sensing type, but I've come out as an N."

> "Last time I did the Indicator I came out as an INTJ – this time I've come out as an ENTP – I'm confused!"

> "On the whole I'd say I'm more Extravert, but there are some situations when I'm definitely Introvert."

> "I used to be very much a Perceiving type, but now I'm more Judging."

...many new practitioners feel they need more strategies up their sleeve!

A recent UK study investigated the proportion of people who decided that the type reported by the MBTI "fitted" for them, after time for consideration. The results indicated that about 76% of people agreed with all four letters of their reported type. Of those who did not, most disagreed on only one letter, and this was most likely to occur when the preference had been reported with a low degree of clarity.

It is clear that the MBTI report provides an excellent starting point for somebody wishing to identify their best fit type. It is equally clear, however, that there will be a significant proportion of people who need time and help to clarify their type. Working with people who are in this situation calls for considerable sensitivity, and represents one of the most important skills a practitioner must acquire.

Type clarification is detective work. It is an art, and like all arts, it includes techniques, but cannot be fully taught. In the end, you will develop your own skills and style through practice. This guide can, however, offer you some suggested avenues which may be useful to explore.

Basic Assumptions

Before going into the strategies, it is worth reiterating some of the assumptions underlying the exploration of type preferences.

First, the theory assumes that there is such a thing as true type, and that this does not change throughout life. However, this is not something that we can observe directly. Nor is it directly assessed by the MBTI. We observe directly our tendencies and behaviour, and these are influenced by type preferences, but not determined by them.

Similarly, the questions on the MBTI ask for responses to simple items which provide clues to the preference, but do not define the preference. For example, it is more typical for an Extravert to "introduce others" than to "be introduced", but there is nothing in the core meaning of Extraversion to say that this will necessarily be the case. Many other influences also affect our tendencies and behaviour. Type clarification is a sifting process, in which the practitioner tries to help the client to isolate their basic, enduring preferences from other influences on their behaviour.

As a very general statement, we may assume that people would behave in ways consistent with the dominant and auxiliary functions* of their true type if they could remove every "should", "must" or "ought" from their mind. However, in practice, this is not a simple matter, and of course these "shoulds" are not necessarily conscious.

To complicate matters further, the way people express their type is expected to change and develop over time. Children and adolescents may be uncertain about their preferences, because these are not yet fully differentiated. On the other hand, as people move into mid life, there is a good probability that they will become more interested in using their tertiary and inferior functions.

Summary of Assumptions**

1. Each of us has a true type, which is assumed to be inborn and unchanging.
2. The way we respond and behave is influenced by our type preferences, and by our current and past environment.
3. In early years, we "discover" and exercise our most preferred functions, and are likely to show behaviour mainly consistent with exercising these preferences. Exceptions to this will occur if something in the environment impedes the expression of a person's type, or if there are situational demands which require that a less-preferred style be adopted.
4. As we move through mid life we may become increasingly drawn to the positive exploration and use of our less preferred functions.
5. The type framework will be much more meaningful and valuable to people if they can uncover their true type than if they attempt to "fit themselves into" a different set of preferences.

**Note that, while many practitioners find that these assumptions are supported by experience, we cannot claim them to be fact. For this reason, we must always respect the client's right to disagree with the assumptions and not accept the model.

*If you are in need of a "refresher" on the dynamics of type (the interplay between dominant, auxiliary, tertiary, and inferior functions), I recommend *Introduction to Type® Dynamics and Development* by Katharine Myers and Linda Kirby (1994).

Steps in Giving Feedback

When giving feedback on the MBTI, practitioners are encouraged to follow a model in which the person first hears a description of the framework and makes an assessment of where they believe they fit, and then goes on to examine their MBTI results. Typical steps in the feedback process would be as follows:

- Remind the client of the purpose of the session and of confidentiality agreements.
- Describe briefly the background of the MBTI and how it can be useful for people.
- Explain the nature of "preference" – for example, by using the analogy of right and left handedness.
- Describe each of the four pairs of opposites, giving examples to illustrate these, and asking the client to self assess as you go along.
- Show the client how he or she has come out on the Indicator – their "Reported Type".
- Show one or more whole type descriptions, for example from *Introduction to Type®* or *Introduction to Type® in Organisations*.
- Help the person to explore areas where they are uncertain about their type and, if possible, to establish a "best-fit" type – that is, the type they believe to be their true type.
- Begin to explore applications of type.

This guide offers strategies for the practitioner to follow at the point where a client has been given a full explanation of the type framework, and is trying to determine for him or herself a best fit type. Quite often, this is very straightforward. The client hears the preferences described, says "I know where I fit in", and then agrees wholeheartedly with the description of the complete four-letter type thus chosen. However, in many cases, things do not go so smoothly.

The strategies in this booklet are for the less straight-forward cases, which represent at least half of the people to whom I give feedback. At first sight, this figure may seem at variance with the research results mentioned earlier, but those results concerned the proportion of people finally agreeing with their reported type. Many may have had doubts along the way!

Cautions

However much one wishes to help someone become clear about their MBTI preferences, and however convinced the practitioner is of the value of this to the client, three things must always be borne in mind:

- Clients (and practitioners) should feel it is perfectly normal and reasonable to end a feedback session without reaching clarity about all, or indeed any, of the preferences. If the client remains interested in clarifying preferences then they may find it helpful to observe their everyday responses over a period of time, and possibly return for a follow up session to discuss their thoughts. The range of exploratory strategies discussed here would be just as applicable to later, follow-up sessions as to an initial feedback session.

- We cannot unequivocally say that the type framework will be useful and meaningful to everyone. It is true that its appeal seems to be very wide, and remarkably general across cultures and settings. Nevertheless, there will no doubt be people for whom it just doesn't "work", for one reason or another. A colleague of mine once put it nicely when she said "remember that people can live long, happy and fulfilled lives without knowing all or any of their MBTI letters!"

- As practitioners, we need to ensure that the exploration process is driven by the client's desire for clarity rather than our own. Some years ago I received a reminder of this fact when feeding back to a reported ESTJ who had some questions about the accuracy of the J. I was most interested in exploring this, and began asking questions about possible work pressures, etc. After a short while, my client was looking impatient, and he said, with admirable directness: "Look, I really don't care that much whether I'm a J or a P – can't we go on to something else!"

To those of us who have found great value in the MBTI, it may seem surprising that someone could "not care" about understanding their preferences, but whatever the potential value of knowing their true type, some clients may not be at a point where they are ready or willing to look at this question in depth. Unless their interest has been engaged in this process, they will be reluctant partners in the search, and the search is not likely to be fruitful. I was grateful to this client for his openness, and wondered whether any previous clients might have been quietly and politely put off by a zeal they did not share.

Here are a few other cautions:

Avoid Biasing Your Descriptions Toward the Type Reported by the Client

If you know the person's reported type before you begin feedback, there can be a seductive temptation to bias your descriptions to make the reported type sound more attractive. Doing so increases the likelihood of quick agreement between reported and self assessed type. Here's a real, not very subtle, example, taken from a new MBTI user practising feedback in a workshop: in front of him was the person's MBTI report, which had come out N. In describing S/N he asked "Do you prefer to use your imagination, or do you find it interesting to look at long lists of data?" Not surprisingly, the person agreed that she preferred to use her imagination!

Resist this temptation firmly. The short term advantage of apparent ease of establishing a best fit type is quite illusory. The individual will get little real benefit if they have an inadequate opportunity to explore the preferences and make a real choice as to where they fit. In addition, some of the richest, most valuable discussions about an individual's type take place when they are *not* immediately clear. Some practitioners have told us that to avoid this problem they ask the client to self assess before they (the practitioner) have scored the MBTI.

Try Not to Bias Your Descriptions Toward Your Own Type

The danger of this will be well-known to all qualified practitioners, so this is just a reminder of the importance of demonstrating equal value for the preferences in your language, your examples and your response to questions. An alternative danger to own type bias is over-compensation – developing such awe and respect for your opposite that you overplay its virtues to the detriment of your own type. There is no simple cure for this problem; however, the best regime is to notice and build up excellent positive, enhancing examples and anecdotes, and to test these on friends and colleagues of the same and opposite type. Most importantly, do not assume that your own personal experiences of type are typical; check with others.

Avoid Using Single "Deciding" Examples

S/N: "How do you cook?"
T/F: "Would you tell the truth or would you be tactful?"

When asked about strategies for clarification of type, less experienced MBTI users often suggest offering example situations and getting the client to choose what they would do. The danger of this is that single "pet" examples may be brought out and used as if they provide the definitive answer. I have heard it suggested that, if someone is struggling with an S/N uncertainty, one should ask the person how they cook. "S's will follow a recipe and weigh out the ingredients precisely. N's will just make it up as they go along."

This is really equivalent to asking a single MBTI question, and assuming that the result will be 100% indicative of type. If it were possible to find individual examples that indicated type with complete consistency, we wouldn't need the MBTI – just four questions (one for each of the pairs of preferences). Isabel Myers tested hundreds of questions and found *none* that could be used in this way. Example situations can be very useful as vehicles for discussion, and it is certainly a good idea to develop a repertoire of anecdotes and examples relevant to your setting. However, responses to one example should not be relied upon as a criterion for someone's preference.

Questions to Ask, Strategies to Follow

Here's a summary of techniques that can help people clarify their type preferences. Each of these will be explored in more depth in the pages that follow.

Opening Questions

Asking people to describe what it is they see in themselves that leads them to say they could fall on either side of the preference pair.

Asking people whether they had a sense of wearing any particular "hat" when they completed the Indicator.

Exploration of "Shoulds," "Musts," and "Oughts"

Asking whether they believe they "should" prefer one or the other side of the preference pair, for any reason.

Asking whether they currently experience pressure from any source to operate in one or the other mode.

Asking whether anything in their background put pressure on them to operate in one or the other mode.

Investigation of Different Situations and Times

Asking how the person's behaviour differs according to the situation. When do they feel "most themselves"?

Asking about different periods of the person's life and how they responded at those times.

Investigating Implications of Dynamics and Development

Describing the dynamic implications of choosing a particular option; emphasising the essential differences between two whole types under consideration.

Looking out for signs that the person is deliberately working on using a less-preferred function.

Use of MBTI Step II, the Expanded Interpretive Report.

Investigating the person's reaction to extreme stress.

Observed Behaviour

Observing and feeding back behaviour during the session itself.

Feedback/experience in group exercises.

Feedback from others.

Finally…

"Keep observing yourself as you …"

"Try it on to see if it fits."

The Strategies in Action

I have listed the strategies on page 6 as separate, perhaps an expression of my ST liking for distinctions and categories. However, in practice they are not separable: a feedback session would move imperceptibly between the strategies and there would seldom be any break or indication that we were changing tack. Each strategy is like a "test probe" and may draw a blank, in which case an entirely new strategy may be adopted. More commonly, one line of questioning blurs into another in a smooth sequence.

Let's take a look at these various strategies in a little more detail, with some examples of how they work in practice. Then I'll take you through a couple of case examples, showing how the strategies blend in with each other and follow from each other.

uncertainty, practitioners often restart their explanations of the preferences without first finding out what has been understood so far. They then run the risk of losing the person's attention by repeating what has been quite well understood, or of making no further headway, because the explanation does not address the area of confusion.

Here are some examples of responses to this question, and how they have helped resolve the individual's uncertainty:

> **E/I:** "Well, listening to your description, on the whole I'd say I'm more like an Introvert, but I do very much like being with people, and I'm very good with people, so I can't decide."

This response suggests that the client may not have fully separated the MBTI meaning of Extraversion/Introversion from the use of the words in everyday language. A first step may be to re-emphasise that difference, focusing on the essence of E/I as a preferred orientation of energy to the outer or inner world, rather than social skills or liking for people.

Opening Questions

> "What do you see in yourself that leads you to say you could be either?"

In my view, this one is almost a "must" in cases where someone is expressing indecision about a particular pair of preferences, and wishes to resolve this uncertainty. It is a simple, open-ended technique which gives you vital information about whether the person has adequately understood the nature of the preferences involved.

In many cases, resolution of the problem amounts to little more than clarifying the explanation of the preferences. However, when a client expresses

S/N: "I know that seeing the big picture, using my imagination, is more like me. I'd identify with almost everything you've said about N. But on the other hand, my work demands a lot of attention to detail, and I think I'm very good at it."

This response provides an excellent opener to a discussion of the possible overlay of type characteristics by the demands of the setting – in this case, job requirements. The person appears to be leaning towards N, and it may be tempting to jump to the conclusion that his confusion is simply caused by a work environment which demands use of Sensing. This would, however, be premature: instead, follow-up questions would explore the individual's experience of using S and N, both in and out of the work setting. If the person not only uses S in his work, but also finds this natural, easy and not fatiguing, then one must be open to the possibility that S is actually his true preference, and that there are other reasons why he identifies with the characteristics of N.

Another question I would ask early in the clarification process is as follows:

"When you filled in the Indicator, did you have a sense of wearing any particular 'hat', ie work, home, 'mother', etc?"

If the answer to this is: "No, I think I was just answering about me in general", then this strategy has probably drawn a blank, and a different approach is needed.

However, quite often, the client will be aware of having had a particular "self" in mind, even if the instructions did not demand this. If this is the case, then further discussion may illuminate the likely effect of answering according to this aspect of self, and whether that is likely to be a good representation of the person's true type.

For example, Claire, who couldn't decide between J and P, responded:

"Well, I filled it in just before I went to collect my daughter from creche. I think I was very much wearing my 'busy mother' hat right then."

Further discussion showed that Claire was aware of "having to be J" in order to fulfil the demands of motherhood combined with a busy career. She regarded P as closer to her natural self, although this side of her wasn't getting much of an airing at the time!

Exploration of "Shoulds," "Musts," and "Oughts"

"Is there any reason why you feel you 'should' be one or the other side of the preference pair?"

This is a very straightforward line of open-ended questioning. One need not speculate as to the origin of the "should", but the question enables clients to ask themselves whether they have a sense that one or the other of the preferences is more acceptable.

Answers that I have had to this question range from work demands, through biases in spouse or friends, to factors in school days or the client's family of origin. Particular peer groups or occupational norms may also have an effect. If the person finds it hard to identify sources of "shoulds", then it may be helpful to ask explicitly about possible pressures now or in the past.

For example, Jane was in the unusual situation of being uncertain about all four of her MBTI preferences. Her reported preferences were ISFJ. Discussion revealed that the religious order to which she belonged had extremely clear norms about what was acceptable behaviour, and that Jane had partially internalised these values. The pressures were towards I, S, F and J. Jane ultimately decided that her true preferences were the exact opposite of these (ENTP), a conclusion that helped her greatly in understanding her difficulty in adjusting to the order.

It is very rare for someone's best-fit type to differ from reported type on all four letters. This is only likely to occur when there are strong constraints (present or past) on the person's freedom to express their preferences. For Jane, these constraints had been powerful and long-standing. Her example is interesting, in that she had accepted and conformed to the constraints over a long period, and yet had never lost the sense that the "real Jane" was different.

Jim, on the other hand, was trying to decide whether ISTJ or INTJ fitted him better. When asked what he thought he "should" be, he was unequivocal.

> "Well, obviously one's supposed to be an S. It's just that N seems so much more appealing..."

I was struck by Jim's assertion that "obviously" S was more socially acceptable. Although Jim had not previously questioned this assumption, when he thought about it he remembered how his father had always demanded to know "the facts" any time they had a discussion, and how scathing he was of anyone who speculated without data. Jim felt that he was probably an intuitive type who had learned to behave like an S for self protection.

Investigation of Different Situations and Times

Asking about different situations – how does the person's behaviour differ according to situation? When do they feel "most themselves"?

Because the MBTI is trying to assess the most "natural you", it is helpful to investigate what people do and how they react when they feel most able to be themselves. Many people can point to situations in which they feel truly free to be their natural selves, although for a few people the question seems meaningless.

Jenny, trying to resolve a T/F uncertainty, said she was most often able to be her natural self at work rather than at home. When she described the situations and activities which truly energised her, it became evident that these tended to involve opportunities to exercise Thinking judgement. Using F, which she had learned to do with a high degree of effectiveness, was associated with times and situations where she felt more constrained.

It's worth noting that, for this woman, work was her least constrained situation. I used to assume that people would be free to be themselves in their non work lives, but cases like these have shown me that this is not necessarily true.

Asking about different periods of the person's life and how they responded at those times

If we accept the premise that type is stable, but its development is dynamic, this strategy becomes a particularly useful one. It can provide a picture of behaviour and responses at different times of the client's life. As well as offering a developmental perspective, it enables the client to look at him or herself from a slight distance, which can often help them to form a clearer picture.

For example Ann, an HR counsellor (aged about 40), was perplexed about whether she preferred E or I.

> "All my friends and colleagues would see me as E. But I just have this strong feeling that my inner world is the one which really fascinates me. I can't really explain or justify it. I seem to show more characteristics of E's: I'm loud, talkative, and spend a lot of time around people."

I asked her about other periods of her life: were there any changes or differences? Would she, for instance, have said the same if asked 10 or 15 years ago? Her answer was very quick and definite.

"I'd certainly have been much more 'I' then", she said. The discussion which followed established that she really did mean I, not just shy, and that she'd internalised a lot of negative feelings about I behaviour from her mother.

> "As a child, I always had my nose in a book. My mother always wanted me to go to parties, and I'd take my book and sit in a corner. It was partly shyness, but mainly that I just found it more interesting to be off in my own imagination than paying attention to what was going on. My mother always thought that this was most peculiar, as if there was something wrong with me because of this."

The discussion helped Ann make sense of the contradiction between her strong feeling that I was her preference, and her outward appearance of being E. For example, she had identified with the E tendency to fill silences in conversation, but now she considered the possibility that this was, in a sense, her mother's discomfort with silence rather than hers. The discussion did not close the question of Ann's E or I preference, but she left feeling happy to "test out" a best-fit type of INTJ.

Investigating Implications of Dynamics and Development

Describing the dynamic implications of choosing a particular option; emphasising the essential differences between two whole types under consideration

The clarification strategies discussed so far have focused on making choices between each of the basic pairs of preferences. For people new to type, discussion of type dynamics may be confusing in the early stages, hence the tendency to remain at the more superficial level of explanation during a first feedback session. However, for some people, an examination of dynamics can provide valuable food for thought in the clarification quest.

For example, Susan was unsure about J/P. A number of the other strategies described above had drawn mixed evidence, and had not come down clearly one way or another. Since Susan was having feedback in preparation for attending an MBTI Qualifying course, it was appropriate to introduce the idea of type dynamics in the clarification process.

Rather than focusing on J/P in isolation, we looked at the implications of J and P for the dynamics of the whole type. Susan had been clear about the first three letters – E, S and F. We examined the essential difference between ESFP and ESFJ.

> "ESFP would suggest that the driving force of your personality is immediate sensory experience in the outer world, while decision making on the basis of feelings and values would be important, but would

> take second place. On the other hand, ESFJ implies that your driving force is deciding and planning on the basis of people's feelings and values, with a secondary process of collecting and gathering factual data to back this up."

Susan was quite definite about the order of her function preferences; for her, it was clear that F was primary, and S secondary. Her greatest delight was planning and organising things in order to please people – for example, organising a pre-Christmas event for the office. She would plan this months in advance – much further ahead than necessary for the sheer joy of doing the planning and making the Feeling decisions involved.

Further discussion suggested that one source of confusion could arise from Susan's difficulty in finding any time for introversion. Thus, rather than showing the usual pattern of dynamics, she appeared to be extraverting both her dominant F and her auxiliary S – hence her recognition in herself of characteristics of the SF type. As always, the situation was not settled for good at the end of the session but, in the process of clarification, we had uncovered an interesting and previously unexplored issue, ie Susan's difficulty in allowing herself any time to pause and reflect.

Investigating the possibility that the person is deliberately working on using a less preferred function

Tony couldn't decide whether J or P fitted him better.

> "I've always been a planner and an organiser. I've always liked to know what I'll be doing and when. But lately I'm learning to be spontaneous, and I'm finding that I really like it!"

This sounds simple: Tony sounds like a J who is developing the ability to use P behaviour at times, and is finding the experiment interesting and enjoyable. This may well be the correct interpretation, but it is not the only one. I would be alert to any signs that the way the person has "always been" was not really comfortable. If the person expresses a sense that their style is imposed rather than natural, then it may be that what they are experiencing represents "coming home" to true type rather than experimenting with a less-preferred side.

Distinguishing between these two interpretations can be particularly difficult, as people often become so intrigued with previously less used functions or attitudes that they feel they are being revealed to themselves for the first time. During such periods of growth and development, the best course is often not to attempt to decide about one's true type, but to live with the ambiguity and see what happens over time.

Use of MBTI Step II (previously called the Expanded Analysis Report)

Some people become confused about their preferences because they recognise that they show most of the typical characteristics of one type, but they see a few things in themselves which seem to point towards the opposite. Step II can be helpful for some such people. This is a computer generated report, based on completion of Form K of the Indicator. Within each of the preferences, Step II has subscales representing the way in which the individual is likely to be expressing his or her type. It can give them a clearer picture of the ways in which their behaviour is typical or atypical of their type.

For example, Melanie felt generally comfortable with a best-fit type of ESTJ, but she was uncertain about J/P. She was interested in Step II, and had the opportunity to complete this and receive feedback.

The results suggested that she showed most of the typical characteristics associated with her type, with one exception. On the J/P subscale "Early Starting–Pressure-Prompted" she came out close to the P end, "Pressure-Prompted". This suggests that Melanie shows a tendency to take on a lot of tasks at once, and to accomplish these by a last-minute rush – a tendency which is usually associated with P. For her, it was helpful to see that she could perfectly well prefer ESTJ, and still not show every expected characteristic of the type.

Discussion of the role of Step II is included here for interest. Please note, however, that for MBTI-qualified practitioners to use Step II, a further one-day qualification course must be attended. Contact OPP for details.

Investigating the person's reaction to extreme stress

Although it would not be the first strategy I would try, for some people it can be helpful and important to explore the possible involvement of the inferior function under stress. This is not a simple matter, however, as type theory predicts that moderate levels of stress would be associated with exaggeration of type, rather than with emergence of the inferior function. This strategy would only be recommended for practitioners who are comfortable and familiar with theory in this area – for example, from reading Naomi Quenk's *Beside Ourselves* or *In the Grip*.

Helen, a participant in a management development workshop, had come out INFP on the Indicator. She had difficulty in identifying with some aspects of the type description, and sought clarification one-to-one.

Because Helen had shown signs of stress and tension, the practitioner mentioned that:

> "Although usually thought of as gentle and accommodating, under extreme stress INFPs can sometimes be quite the opposite, and may come across as very critical and even judgemental."

To Helen, this was a revelation, and on which was accompanied by great relief. She had been aware of being seen as aggressive and critical, and had been puzzled by her own behaviour. Understanding that this was a predictable reaction for an INFP under stress, and "in the grip" of inferior T, both confirmed that these preferences were a good fit for her and reduced her confusion and distress.

Observed behaviour

Observing and feeding back behaviour during the session itself

Behaviour during the feedback session often provides clues to the client's preference. It can be very helpful to reflect examples of such behaviour when they occur, as the immediacy of such examples can bring the concepts alive in a way that hypothetical instances may not. Here again, caution is in order. Clients are often susceptible to being led by the practitioner, and to regarding him or her as an expert judge. Therefore it is essential that practitioners confine themselves to commenting upon pieces of *behaviour* and not passing any *judgements* on the person.

Type-related differences in communication style can often be observed during the feedback session, particularly on the E/I and S/N dimensions. For example, it is characteristic of people preferring Introversion that they pause for a moment, often looking down, before replying to a question.

People preferring Extraversion tend to begin their replies at once, developing their answers as they speak. People preferring Sensing tend to ask for concrete examples, and are likely to provide more specific detail when explaining things. People preferring Intuition are more inclined to use global concepts, and to talk in terms of possibilities.

If the client is wrestling with a particular pair of preferences, and the content or style of his or her communication seems more like one of these, I may choose to reflect this, with care. For example, if E/I were in doubt, I might reflect my observations as follows:

> "You know, during this session, when I ask you a question, I notice that you typically stop and look down for a moment, and then respond. You seem to take time to reflect before you speak. In that respect your style seems more like that of an Introvert. What do you make of that?"

Further exploration would establish whether the person agreed with the observation, and whether this behaviour was, indeed, representative of their general behaviour, or a particular reaction to the situation. Such observations never settle the question of a client's preference, but they can provide valuable data for consideration.

Feedback from others

In a similar vein, for some people, feedback from others can be a useful source of information for them to consider. This is likely to be especially helpful for people whose level of self awareness is relatively low. This could come from fellow participants in a group event, or could be requested from friends or work colleagues.

Of course, people's feedback tends to be based primarily on outward appearance, especially if it comes from short acquaintance. Nevertheless, it can provide useful information about the impression one makes on others.

For example, Frances came out INTJ, but saw herself as very practical and realistic. This made her slightly uncertain about her preference on the S/N pair. She asked for feedback from a colleague with a preference for S. One of her comments was as follows:

> "I can't help noticing that you often leave out words when you're writing sentences. It's as if your mind is moving ahead in terms of ideas, so that you're no longer focusing on what's in front of you. Another thing which amuses me is the way you pass things on to me with no indication of what I'm meant to do with them. Sometimes I find this a bit frustrating, although I've learned to live with it."

This feedback helped Frances to distinguish between her natural drive to create logical order, an expression of her extraverted Thinking function, and her much less strong drive to attend to detail and specifics. She concluded that INTJ did, indeed, fit her best.

Experiences in group exercises

If the MBTI is being used as part of a group event of some sort, then people can often use their experience in certain exercises to help them clarify their preferences. There are numerous examples of exercises which tend to "bring out" each of the preferences, including the following:

> **E/I**: Type alike groups come up with questions to ask their opposites, and have a chance to ask and answer the questions.
>
> **S/N**: Groups of S's and N's look at a complex picture and discuss what they see in it.
>
> **T/F**: Groups of T's and F's discuss and report on questions concerned with appreciation or recognition.
>
> **J/P**: Participants line themselves up on a continuum from "I get my work done before I play" to "I can play any time", and discuss why they chose their position.

The point of these exercises is not to provide "the answer" to someone's question. However, the experience of working with others of supposedly similar or different types can often help people to become clearer about themselves. For example, Peter was trying to decide whether T or F suited him better. He chose to work with the T's during the "appreciation" exercise, and afterwards said: "That settles it! I'm definitely looking at things in a different way from them!" He found himself feeling much more at home as he listened to presentations made by the F groups. This experience made him much more confident of his preference; however, I encouraged him to use the experience as one more piece of data, rather than taking it as the "decider".

Finally…

"Keep observing yourself as you…"

As mentioned at the beginning of this booklet, it is perfectly acceptable to end a clarification session without reaching certainty about the client's preferences. It is often helpful for the person to have some guidance about what to look for in themselves, in order to continue the process of exploring their preferences. Here are a few suggestions:

If E and I are in doubt, I would suggest that the person observe how they find themselves processing ideas or experience. If they've had an interesting idea or experience, is their first reaction: "Who can I talk to about this?", or is it: "I need some time to think about this"?

Alternatively, if they have some time for private reflection, do they experience this as restful and re-energising, or do they find that they are becoming restless, seeking some kind of external stimulation? Many E's, especially those whose work demands a lot of interaction, recognise that they need quiet time for balance. On the other hand, when they observe their own reactions, they often report that it is easy to overlook this need, and that they have to remind themselves to take time out from interaction.

If S and N are in doubt, I would suggest that the person observe what tends to excite and interest them when discussing a problem. Do they become energised when developing general ideas and concepts, or do they get more engaged when thinking or talking about how things would really work? If a new concept is introduced, do they find themselves immediately trying to understand what this would mean in a specific situation, or do they find themselves interested in the concept itself and its potential ramifications and connections?

Alternatively, some people find that their Perceiving preferences are most obvious when observing what they become aware of when reading books or watching films. Are they mainly drawn to the story "as it is", or do they find themselves drawn to connections, ideas and associations?

If T and F are in doubt, I would again suggest that the person observe how they tend to approach problems, both in and out of work. Do they find themselves focusing primarily on the objectively-defined task, and having to consider impact on feelings in a deliberate way, if at all? Or do they find themselves "naturally" looking at the issue in terms of values and impact, and having to push themselves if they are to take a more detached standpoint? Similarly, if they need to help someone or give them feedback, do they more automatically focus on the "what" ("What is the problem?", "What messages do I need to convey?") or the "who" ("Who am I trying to help?", "What does this individual need?")?

If J and P are in doubt, I would suggest that the person notice how they find themselves approaching their work and projects, particularly when they are free to decide on an approach. Do they find themselves keeping open and exploring where the process leads? Or do they like to decide on their objectives and work towards these in a goal-directed fashion? Do they find themselves pushing for closure and decisions, or do they find themselves resisting making decisions earlier than necessary?

"Try it on to see if it fits."

None of the preceding strategies is likely to come up with a definitive answer as to a client's preferences. However, at the end of a feedback session the client may well have come to a tentative view about his or her best-fit type. From this point, the best approach is for the client to live with the type they believe to fit them, and to see how this feels.

The term best-fit is a good description for how it feels to identify one's true preferences. There is a sense in which "wearing" these preferences feels comfortable, and seems to increase one's freedom of movement. On the other hand, living with the wrong best-fit type is likely to feel at best as if it takes you nowhere, and at worst like wearing a straitjacket!

Remember Jim (mentioned on page 9), who came out ISTJ, but felt that INTJ fitted him better? At the end of the session, I suggested to Jim that he try using his Intuition, by going with his hunches in a few safe situations. When he returned for a follow-up session, he recounted the following:

> *"The day after our last session I encountered the Chief Executive, and he asked me a question about what we should do on a particular project. I had an immediate and strong hunch about the answer, but normally I would have hesitated, and gone off to ferret out some facts to back up my ideas. This time I decided to go ahead and tell him. It felt great!"*

Discussing important matters with the Chief Executive was not exactly what I'd had in mind as a "safe" situation! However, Jim was delighted with the way it had gone, and there were evidently no adverse consequences. For him, it was as if the floodgates were opened as soon as he gave himself permission to use Intuition.

It was interesting to see that Jim's "release" in terms of type was mirrored by an apparent release of physical tension. When I first saw him, he would twist himself into all kinds of strange knots while we were talking, seeming literally wound up. Because he seemed to be holding so much tension, I suggested that he try the Alexander Technique. He took to it with considerable enjoyment, and there seemed to be a pleasing synergy between this, which helped him physically relax, and his newfound freedom to "be himself".

Before we met, Jim had been perceived as effective, but as lacking in self assurance, especially when dealing with more senior managers. Soon after, he began to be seen as much more confident, and he was promoted within a few months. The ease and confidence with which he operated "as an INTJ" convinced him, and me, that this was a good fit for him.

Case Examples

The following are some more extended case examples showing how the clarification process might proceed.

June – ENTJ or ENFP?

June, a fairly senior manager about 40 years old, asked for a one-to-one counselling session during an MBTI Qualifying workshop, because she felt very unhappy about the way she had come out on the MBTI, but couldn't decide exactly what the problem was.

"I've come out ENTJ," she said to me, "and I know that if I asked anyone, they'd say 'yes, that's you' – I know it's how I behave. But I hate it! I don't really think it's me."

"OK... so, first of all, are there some parts you are especially unhappy with, and some parts you are more comfortable with?"

"Yes," said June, "I'm pretty happy with the E, and with the N. It's the T and the J that I have trouble with."

"OK. What do you see in yourself which makes you less sure about the T and the J?"

"Well it's not my behaviour! I know that I behave like a typical TJ – making tough decisions, being very objective, keeping my personal feelings out of decisions, being organised and planned. But I just don't like those aspects of myself."

"...and earlier on you said you didn't think the type was really 'you'. Does that mean that, as well as not liking these TJ things, they also don't, in some sense, feel like 'you'?"

"No, they don't. And yet, I've always been like that. It's not as if it's just a response to a work situation. I'm like that at home as well."

This was very interesting to me, because June had come across, since the start of the workshop, as a very tense person, ill at ease with herself. From what she had said so far, I began to hypothesise that, for some reason or other, she was fighting her "true nature". I did not, at this point, have a strong feeling of what that true nature might be.

"So you're saying that you behave like this all the time, but it doesn't feel like the real you? Is that really true, or are there some situations where you behave differently? Particularly, are there any situations where you feel more able to be 'yourself?'"

June thought for a moment, and then said:

"You know, I think I do occasionally feel like I get a glimpse of the real me – not very often, but with a certain group of girlfriends..."

"So tell me a bit more about those times... and about the you that comes out at those times."

"They're very spontaneous times... nothing is planned – we just do whatever we feel like. It's one of the few times of my life when I feel it's OK for me not to be the one in control."

"Has that been an important theme for you – being in control?"

At this point, I saw a change come over June. A look of pain passed briefly across her face, and it appeared that she was struggling with a thought or memory which she kept from her consciousness most of the time. She regained her composure with some difficulty and then said:

> "Being in control has always seemed absolutely essential. Not being in control seems terrifying, and I know why, too…"

At this moment, I was aware that if we delved deeper, we would be hitting against things that were extremely emotionally charged. I used to be surprised at the capacity of an MBTI feedback session to touch deep parts of people. I should not have been surprised, because these sessions deal with the issue of who you believe yourself to be as a person, and with some of the reasons why you may not have been allowed to "be yourself". Naturally, some of these reasons go pretty deep, and are connected with ancient and powerful emotions.

It is a judgement call as to whether it is appropriate to persist, but June seemed to be inviting further exploration.

> "You know why…?" I said.

She looked up at me, her face changed from that of a cool, confident manager, to a vulnerable, searching expression. I felt she was checking to see if she could trust me. The next moment she could close up again, or she could decide to go on.

> "Do you mind all this… do you mind me going on about myself in this way? It must be really boring for you."

> "It's fine – I'm interested – as long as you're happy to go on."

> "OK," she said.

She went on to tell me her story, which took us back to her childhood. It was a sad tale of a frightened little girl growing up surrounded by violence and alcoholism. Spontaneity had become bound up with lack of control. Lack of control went with alcohol. Alcohol went with violence. The only safe course was to be in complete control at all times.

From this point on, no new "strategies" were needed. We had hit upon a rich seam of highly relevant material, and one which June was more than willing to explore.

Control was not the only issue in her young life. Emotion also became highly dangerous, both because it was associated with lack of control, and because her feelings were frequently abused and ridiculed. For self-protection she had learned to retreat behind a tough stance, and to win arguments by unassailable logic.

June had become quite successful at sustaining the dual disciplines of control and of unemotionality. As an adult, in the business world, she took advantage of this training, and had achieved considerable success and a reputation as a tough, uncompromising manager. But always at a cost.

At the end of our session, June concluded that her TJ behaviour could well have been a product of her early stresses, reinforced later by the career she chose. She cried during the session, as she described her childhood, but she finished looking bright, optimistic, and more open than at any time during the workshop.

> "Do you mean to say that it might actually be OK for me to be an ENFP?" she asked me, with eager energy.

> "Absolutely – if it's right for you. Why not try it on for a while and see how it feels?"

June was ready to end the session then, telling me that she felt a little scared, but incredibly excited. The energy and excitement which accompanied her decision to "try out" ENFP suggested to me that she was on the right track. This release of energy on "coming home" to true type is especially characteristic for people like June, whose true selves have been negated and distorted by experience, but who are aware enough to know this, and ready to face their fears.

The epilogue to this tale was a brief but happy note I received from June about three weeks later. It said, simply: "Thank you for releasing me from ENTJ!" The signature was hard to read, and for a moment I couldn't think who it was from, and then I realised and smiled. Clearly June had enjoyed her trial period as an ENFP! Just for the record, I should mention, of course, that ENTJ is a fine type for "real" ENTJs, but for June it represented all the repression and self denial of her life.

Matthew – ENFJ or ENTJ?

Matthew completed the MBTI as part of an individual development programme. During his feedback session he readily identified with preferences for E, N and J but felt torn about T/F. As usual, I first asked him:

> "What do you see in yourself that makes you say you could be either?"

Matthew replied:

> "I know that I'm very logical in the way I make decisions, and I can certainly make tough decisions, but I do care very much about people, and I try to think about what matters to them."

This reply reveals two possible sources of confusion. Firstly, I might inadvertently have given the impression that people preferring Thinking are uncaring. Secondly, Matthew might not have fully understood the notion of preference as something which is not absolute, but a matter of ease, naturalness and order. My response was as follows:

> "Perhaps I gave you the impression that only F's care about people. If I did, that's quite wrong. T and F are decision-making processes, and are concerned with what tends to come first and most naturally as criteria in decisions. T's tend first and most naturally to consider decisions from the outside, and to apply logic to the objective situation. It may take a more deliberate effort for them to put themselves inside a situation and consider it from the standpoint of impact on people. The reverse is true for F's; they will more naturally evaluate situations in terms of the impact on those involved, and may find it harder to 'step out' and consider the situation from the standpoint of objective logic. Whichever is your preference, you are likely to make at least some use of both processes, but the preference tends to show itself in which of these 'just seems to happen' and which needs to be more deliberately brought into the picture."

Note that this clarification was intended to be neutral as to the resolution of the individual's uncertainty. Although the initial response indicated some misunderstanding of the implications of having a T preference, it did not mean that Matthew was a T. Further discussion was needed in order to move forward. On hearing this explanation, Matthew went on to say:

> "I do think about impact on people, but you see, with all the problems of the UK economy at the moment, there's little I can do about this. We don't have the power to give promotions, or increase people's salaries, so I feel a bit helpless."

I chose to take the opportunity to feed back Matthew's behaviour. As mentioned before, this can be a very useful strategy. Let me say again, though, since it is so vital, that the client must remain free to say, firstly, whether the interpretation of the behaviour was accurate and, secondly, whether the behaviour displayed was typical of them and representative of their natural self.

Here's how I responded to Matthew:

> "That's interesting. What you just described sounds to me like an example of T reasoning because, while you are clearly concerned with people's welfare, you appear to be looking at the situation from the outside, and thinking of it in objective terms – what you can and can't do for them in terms of money or promotion. Using Feeling in that situation would involve putting yourself in their position, and asking: 'What would have an impact on them?'; 'What really matters to them?'; 'What would I really care about if I were in their shoes?' It might be that you would come to the same conclusion – that the only things that matter are money or promotion. Or you might conclude that, despite your inability to alter these objective factors, there are still things you can do."

At this, a look of comprehension spread across his face. It was a look which betrayed a deeper comprehension than the mere understanding of my words.

> "Ah," he said, "I think perhaps I now understand what my wife's been trying to tell me for a long time."

In this case, Matthew recognised the behaviour he had just displayed in the session as typical of himself in many situations, and went on to describe, with some excitement, anecdotes from his past which he had found puzzling, and which now fell into place. He ended the session comfortable with a best fit of ENTJ.

Sally – ESTP or ENTP?

In my own case, when I first completed the MBTI, I reported ENTP, and it seemed a reasonable enough fit. However, it never seemed to do anything for me or help me to understand my reactions.

I had particular doubts as to where I fitted on the S/N index. I felt that I was able to handle complex, theoretical subjects, and that I enjoyed the challenge of dealing with abstract matters. On the other hand, I recognised many aspects of S – seeing myself as observant of everyday detail, having a good memory for facts, and finding it easy and relaxing to focus on immediate practical realities. After some time of struggling with this question on my own, a fellow trainer suggested we talk the issue through properly. I found the session so helpful that it provided a good part of the motivation to write this booklet.

My colleague, Catherine, asked whether I felt that I "should" be S or N. I didn't hesitate.

> "I really feel I should be N – that to be S would be inferior. Anybody can learn facts – there's nothing very clever about that. It's figuring out what the facts mean that's difficult."

Catherine's questioning helped me to identify a variety of sources for my feeling that "N was better". One of these was my family of origin, but I had also experienced occupational group pressure, since my subject (psychology) typically attracts a very high proportion of Intuitive types. I had worked very hard to grasp complex theories, and had become quite adept at doing this. In retrospect, I realised that the way I would do this was by taking the concepts and figuring out what they would mean in specific examples. If I could not do this, I would find the concepts frustrating and meaningless. I developed a particular talent for picking out the flaws in an argument, when this was subjected to rigorous analysis.

A final source of confusion was the portrayal, in some of the type literature, of S types as non-intellectual. Academic success had come relatively easily to me, and I had never had difficulty in learning from written materials.

As we talked, I realised that I was getting tired of working with concepts, and I no longer wanted to expend the energy necessary to work continuously at this level. I was losing patience with theoretical approaches and becoming much more interested in seeing things work in practice. Fortunately, rather by chance my work had recently taken a turn which was much more practical and applied in nature.

During our discussion, I realised that I had often felt unconfident about who I was meant to be, and that I had always looked for admired figures as role models. I had never fully valued my S abilities, tending to feel that if something came easily, it couldn't be worth very much. For example, for a time I took up painting as a hobby, and found I was able to produce quite attractive, realistic representations of still life arrangements. I gave it up, however, saying that the work "lacked imagination" and wasn't worth doing. At university, I focused so much on grasping theory that for a while I was in danger of not learning enough facts. However, a helpful tutor suggested that it was important for me to include facts in my essays, and to learn some facts for the purpose of passing exams. I then set myself to the task of absorbing copious amounts of information in a short period of time, and found it fairly easy and quite enjoyable.

I concluded that I wanted to "try out" ESTP. This decision was associated with an immediate rush of excitement and energy, as seems to be characteristic of people discovering their true preferences. I felt a sense of release and new freedom to enjoy aspects of myself which I had tended to undervalue. It was not that I now devalued the N skills I had worked so hard to develop, but I now felt entitled to stop forcing myself to use N all the time. After a week of experimenting with "being an S", I was confident that this was, indeed, my true type.

By contrast, when I later began to wonder whether T or F might fit me better, I tried out living as an ESFP for a week. That one week was quite enough to convince me that, much as I valued F, it was not my true preference.

Conclusion

I once saw a piece of graffiti on a wall in Brixton. It was surrounded by other graffiti, much of it violent in content and directed against one or other group in society. I thought this piece must have been put there by the "MBTI Liberation Front." It read simply:

"BE YOURSELF!"

The MBTI provides a wonderful framework for discovering who that self really is. My own personal experience, as well as the experience of numerous clients, has confirmed the value of taking time to explore where one's natural preferences lie. As a partner in this process, someone who asks the right questions and really tries to understand the responses can be invaluable. It is my hope that this booklet will help practitioners as they build up a repertoire of questions and strategies to guide people in this process of discovery.

References

Myers, I B, Kirby, L K, & Myers, K D. 1994. *Introduction to Type®*. Fifth Edition. Palo Alto, CA: CPP.

Hirsh, S K, & Kummerow, J M. 1990. *Introduction to Type® in Organisations.* Palo Alto, CA: CPP.

Myers, K D, & Kirby, L K. 1994. *Introduction to Type® Dynamics and Development.* Palo Alto, CA: CPP.

Quenk, N L. 1993. *Beside Ourselves: Our Hidden Personality in Everyday Life.* Palo Alto, CA: Davies Black Publishing.

Quenk, N L. 1996. *In the Grip: Our Hidden Personality.* Palo Alto, CA: CPP.

All the above materials are available from OPP.